A Death in the Family

The Loss of a Child

By

PATRICK CAMPBELL

ISBN 978-1515238577

Published by
P.H. Campbell
82 Bentley Avenue
Jersey City, NJ 07304
(201) 434-2432
pathcampbe@aol.com

BOOKS BY PATRICK CAMPBELL

A Molly Maguire Story (Revised Edition)

The Death of Franklin Gowen

The World Trade Center: The 1993 Attack: Unanswered Questions

Mad Dog Coll: And His Wife Lottie

The Famine Years In Northwest Donegal: 1845 – 1850

Napper Tandy & William Burton Conyngham: Lords of Burtonport

Memories of Dungloe, County Donegal: 1940 – 1960 (Revised Edition)

Ghosts?: Four Strange Stories

A Death in the Family: The Loss of a Child

Hurricane!!: The Night of the Big Wind: Donegal 1839

The Incident on the Pier Road: A Horror Story

Dedicated to Padraic

The death of a child is the worst experience that can happen to any parent, and when the child dies suddenly and violently the experience is all the more devastating.

It is an event that no parent completely recovers from.

Much has been written about "closure" and "healing" in connection with the aftermath of such a tragedy, but for many, if not for most parents, there is no closure, and there is only limited healing. At best, there is only the learned ability to endure the pain and to hope that time will make it more bearable.

My wife Eileen and I lost our thirteen-year-old son Padraic on December 5, 1985, and hardly a day goes by since then that we do not think of him. He was killed by a drunken driver who fled the scene and left him to die at the side of the road.

Eileen and I had been aware that tragedies like this could and did happen, but we were unaware of the con- sequences for any family that suffered such a loss. Several months before Padraic's death we learned that an Irish family who belonged to our church had lost a nine- year-old daughter to cancer, and even though we went to the wake and sympathized with them at the time, we were not aware of what the parents were going through.

I spoke to the father briefly and I told him that I had difficulty understanding how he could cope with such a loss, and he told me that he had no idea how he was going to survive the tragedy, but that he had to be strong for his son, who was taking the loss of his sister very badly.

Three months later, when my son was being waked, he was one of the first to walk into the funeral home accompanied by his wife and son, and by then I knew what he had gone through: this incredible pain of the loss, and an inability to understand why this tragedy had come to a family who had enjoyed life so much.

* * *

1985 had been a busy year for all four members of the Campbell family.

I had a full time job with the Port Authority of New York and New Jersey marketing the World Trade Center; and I had two part time jobs—one of them writing two weekly columns for the *Irish Echo Newspaper*—the other researching a book on the Molly Maguires.

Eileen had decided to sell real estate in Jersey City and had enrolled in Saint Peters University in Jersey City to earn the credits that would enable her to acquire a license.

Padraic was in his last year in Saint Aloysius Grammar School in Jersey City, where he had been on the basketball team and the track team, and had applied to Regis, a Jesuit high school in New York. He had high hopes of being admitted.

And Nora was beginning to display a major talent for running on the Saint Aloysius track team and in later years would become a star of the team.

1985 was also the year that I fulfilled a dream I had for years: to go on a road trip across the United States to California, driving west on the southern route and coming back on the northern route. Padraic and Nora were very excited about the prospect of the trip, but Eileen wanted no part of an 8,000 mile road trip and said she would rather spend a month with her parents in Ireland while we spend thirty days in our car travelling from town to town across the country. So, we parted company for a month, but it worked out very well for all involved: Eileen loved spending quality time with her relatives in Ireland; we visited every attraction all across the country and back.

In a way the trip was a blessing because Padraic kept saying that he was having a "trip of a lifetime" and at the time I had no way of knowing that this would indeed be the only road trip we would ever go on again.

But in the week before Padraic's death there had been some stress in the family: Padraic wanted me to buy him a new skateboard, which were all the rage among teenage boys in 1985

Eileen did not like skateboards because she thought they were dangerous, but many of Padraic's friends had skateboards and I saw no harm in getting him a brand new one which I thought were far less dangerous than the old skateboards he sometimes borrowed from his friends.

He was to die on that skateboard and his death added an element of guilt to my grief, because I thought that if I had not bought him the skateboard he would still be alive.

But I found some comfort from the fact that neither Eileen nor anyone else seemed to blame me for my son's death. More than one person told me that I was only trying to be good to my son by buying him the skateboard, not trying to kill him, but the feelings of guilt were very difficult to shake, especially since Eileen had been so opposed to skateboards in the first place.

Our relatives and friends were also devastated and most of them had no idea how to console us.

We did not blame them for that. When Padraic died we went to live in a new reality that bore little resemblance to the reality we had lived in previously.

Until that point in time we had endured the "normal" concerns of family life: the everyday problems connected with living a fast paced life, with every member of the family involved in a wide variety of activity outside the home, and four unique individuals making the compromises needed for them to live together.

Suddenly we were living in a reality where all previous activities seemed meaningless, and our only awareness was a deep sense of shock and pain that did respond to the kind words of friends.

The well-meaning efforts of friends and relatives, which they thought would make us feel better, only made us more depressed.

The concepts that seemed to make sense to me in my previous life seemed absurd...ridiculous...nonsense...in the world I now lived in.

An example of this occurred when a close friend came to me the day after Padraic was killed and gave me some advice on how I should cope with the disaster: he said I should focus on the thirteen good years I had with my son and not focus on the abrupt ending of his life. He said I should "celebrate" Padraic's life and dwell on all the wonderful things he had achieved in his thirteen short years.

He believed if I were to accept the reality of what had happened, I would understand that this was Padraic's allotted time on this world and that I had been given the gift of his company by God for that length of time.

He told me that I had been a very good father to Padraic and that I should never think for a moment that his death was in any way a reflection on me.

I suppose this man thought this was a very sensible approach to the tragedy and I am sure he thought it made a great deal of sense to him.

But as I looked at him I wondered if he would take the same approach if he lost one of his own children, and somehow I thought he would not. Indeed I knew he would have been as devastated as I was, and if anyone had given him the advice he had just given me he would have thought that that person was extremely insensitive.

The reality was that any enjoyment I might have had at the thirteen years of Padraic's life was buried in the pain of the knowledge that I would never enjoy a moment of his company again. And I kept thinking that I was the only father in the whole United States at that particular moment whose son was killed on a skateboard. The only consolation I had was the thought that kept repeating itself in my head: I kept telling myself "Padraic is suffering no pain; I am the one who is suffering."

But I had enough self-control not to tell my friend what I really thought of his advice, and he probably left my home thinking he had performed a good deed.

But this incident gave me an insight into the fact that the vast majority of adults have no idea of the pain endured by a parent who has lost a child, and have no idea what to say to such a parent.

Losing a child is very different from losing any other member of a family. I lost my parents, and have buried sisters and brothers, and while there was grief at every one of those deaths, the loss of a child is an entirely different species of grief that cannot be compared to any other bereavement. It inflicts a psychological earthquake on the parent that can never be comprehended by a person who has not lost a child.

A priest who came to visit us was very kind but just as insensitive as my friend, and I thought at the time that he should have known better how to comfort a grieving parent. But as I thought about it later I concluded that the priest would have had no personal experience of losing a child either, so how would he understand the reality of the situation.

The priest's approach was to tell us that he was convinced that Padraic was now in Heaven, and that we should not mourn him but celebrate the fact that he was now up there with God. He said God must have wanted him and therefore he came and got him, and that it was a great honor to have been chosen by God.

As I listened to him I thought that only a bachelor who had never fathered a child, or been loved by a child, would think that such an argument would make any sense to grieving parents.

The irony of this approach was that while he thought it was designed to draw Eileen and me closer to God, it had the opposite effect on me because I thought God had no right to take our child and break our hearts in the process. His little sermon was the type of approach that drove some parents away from God: it did not bring them closer to Him.

My extended family had no knowledge about our state of mind either and were equally incompetent about giving advice.

One relative thought we should consider adopting a son to replace Padraic, and I was very blunt in my response: I told him we had not lost a pet dog that could be replaced by a pup. I said Padraic was unique and as such was irreplaceable. After that he did not bring the subject up again.

None of the people who gave this advice intended to do us any harm. They did not know how to console us and they offered the advice that seemed sensible to them, not knowing they were only making matters worse.

Losing a child is a unique experience and only those who have lost children know how to console another grieving parent.

The ideal approach to a grieving parent is very simple: be a very good listener, because the parents feel compelled to talk about their loss and vent the agony that is overwhelming them. Only give advice if you are a bereaved parent yourself and have been down that road and know what to say...and what not to say.

* * *

The two-day wake at a funeral parlor in Bayonne, NJ, was very difficult to endure. Eileen and I had a wide circle of friends and all of them showed up for the wake.

I had numerous friends and acquaintances from my association with my work at the World Trade Center and *The Irish Echo* newspaper and this drew large volumes of people to the funeral home. Eileen was a real estate agent and had a wide circle of friends and business acquaintances and they all showed up. Nora's class at school came to sympathize, and all of Padraic's friends from school and the boy scouts turned up in force.

Then the very fact that a child had died violently attracted people to sympathize with us who might not have turned up if Padraic had been an adult.

In all, lines of people came to pay their respects for two days and it was very hard to keep our composure when we were confronted by so many people, many of whom greeted us while in a very emotional state.

The only time I nearly lost my composure was when an old friend named Charles Comer showed up with Paddy Maloney, leader of the Chieftains, the Irish traditional group. I had written many reviews of Chieftains concerts in the Irish Echo, and when Comer, who was Maloney's press agent, told Paddy about what had happened he said he wanted to attend the wake and sympathize with me.

But when Comer told me Maloney had brought his flute along and wanted to play some Irish melodies in Padraic's honor I almost broke down and I told Comer I just did not want him to do that - that I had brought Padraic to a dozen Chieftains' concerts and that listening to Maloney play in the funeral parlor would bring back a flood of memories and I just could not endure it. So, Maloney did not play.

I do not know what Comer told Maloney but I hoped he told him I appreciated the gesture, even if I could not accept the gift of his music. Maloney's heart was in the right place and I know he thought he was making a gesture that would be welcomed by me.

There was a few other incidents at the wake that were unsettling, but they did not have the potential impact that the possibility of hearing Paddy Maloney's music had.

Later, a woman came up to me and handed me her card: she said she was a psychiatrist and had been at the scene of the accident and that I would need therapy. She asked me if I wanted to make an appointment, but I just turned on my heel and walked away. I had heard of ambulance chasers but this was the first time I had ever heard of a psychiatrist drumming up business in a funeral parlor. It was unbelievable.

Towards the end of the evening a pompous little man in an ill-fitting suit walked past all those waiting in line to sympathize with us and presented himself to Eileen and me. He said he came to represent a member of the Jersey City Council who represented our district and to offer the councilman's sympathy to us.

I was speechless. Several questions came to mind but I did not ask them. Questions such as—why hadn't the councilman come himself?; why did he send a pompous little person like this who thought he was on a very important mission; and why did the councilman not have the common sense to know that in a situation like this sympathies should only be expressed in person. But I said nothing and the little man strutted off—mission accomplished.

On the second evening of the wake a police lieutenant in the Jersey City Police Department, who had arrested the man who had killed my son and locked him up in the Hudson County Jail, came to me and told me that the man arrested and charged with vehicular homicide had been released from jail on low bail and the charges against him reduced to leaving the scene of an accident. He said the District Attorney had reduced the charges because there were no witnesses to support the charges against him.

He said he was distressed by this but it was the District Attorney's call and the police could do nothing about it. I made no response to him because I could not focus on anything else at that moment.

But days later, when I learned more about the man, I would think it obscene that this person, who was an illegal alien who had killed a child while driving intoxicated in a car that had no insurance or registration could be released on such low bail and walk away a free man.

I appreciated all the outpouring of sympathy and it provided a temporary buffer for Eileen and me against dwelling on the terrible reality that we had lost our son, even if this relief lasted for only a few hours at the wake.

As long as we were surrounded by people we were shielded from thinking about the child who lay silently in the open coffin beside us.

But we knew that all those people who had reached out to us would go back to their homes and their normal life and we would be left alone with the pain of our loss and with no way to lessen it. All we could hope for was that time would give us some relief.

* * *

I stayed out of work for two weeks after Padraic's death and spent some of the time in Florida going from one amusement park to another, hoping to keep eight-year-old Nora's mind off the loss of her brother and to prevent us from sitting at home brooding. But that did not work out the way we had planned.

I had thought initially that it would help to be with crowds of people, but then I saw that the Disney complex and all the other amusement parks were full of parents and their children and every time I saw a thirteen-year- old boy walking with his father I thought of Padraic.

But in those two weeks I also became aware that the other two members of my family were also suffering from this loss, although none of us were able to express our grief, and all three of us retreated into a moody silence. I knew that "healing" was going to take a very long time.

After that we retreated back to New Jersey and tried as best we could to pick up the pieces of our life again but it was not easy.

* * *

We were helped, however, by the kindness of our neighbors who reached out to help us as much as they could.

On the first day Nora was due back in school we sat silently around the breakfast table, again thinking of Padraic. They had always walked down the street and along Westside Avenue to school together. Now he was not there for her.

Eileen was about to tell her that she was going to walk her to school when the doorbell rang, and when I opened the door there was Colin Rigby, a nine-year-old neighbor, who said he had come to walk Nora to school. He did this for the rest of the school year.

Several weeks later, after a heavy fall of snow, I looked out the front window and there was Colin shoveling the snow from our sidewalk, a chore Padraic usually handled.

From time to time we would get visits from Padraic's friends who would just stop by to see how we were. One in particular, John Airey, would stay for an hour, and it was very comforting to know our son had not been forgotten.

Padraic had been in the boy scouts and the group organized a special Mass in his memory, and as a result of all this support, we managed to get through the first few weeks in one piece.

* * *

I went back to the World Trade Center after the Florida trip and the first several days at work were the hardest of my life. More than once I felt like walking out the door and going home.

Many of my coworkers were at the wake and they welcomed me back warmly; others that I had been friendly with for years ignored me and never mentioned my loss.

Some of those who had ignored me at first came around months later and talked to me about my loss and apologized   for not coming around sooner. One said:

"I really did not know what to say to you. I have a son of my own...."

The head of my department who I had worked with for twenty years never once mentioned my loss.

The worst part of my day was attending meetings with a score of people, because typically at these meetings people cracked jokes and talked in a light-hearted way, and since my mind was frozen with grief, I could barely tolerate the laughter.

I also had a major problem with the Christmas music that was being piped into all the public areas of the World Trade Center. I could not tolerate the "happy" lyrics and music.

* * *

I was obviously in a very bad state of mind, although I never talked to anybody at work about how I was feeling.

However, one day I was approached by a woman named Lois Bohovesky—an actress who staged puppet shows every Christmas at the World Trade Center. She asked me to have lunch with her because there was something important that she wanted to talk to me about.

I liked Lois because we had a professional relationship for years: she did a great job entertaining groups of children who were visiting the Trade Center; I promoted her little acting troupe to the media. I agreed to go to lunch with her.

When we took our seats in one of the restaurants at the World Trade Center, Lois looked me in the eye and told me I was in a state of shock and needed help.

"I can see it in your eyes," she said.

"Nobody in your office has a clue about the destructive nature of what has happened to you. They don't know how to talk to you. And many believe that it is best not to bring up your loss at all because they think it will only upset you.

"You really got to get involved with people who know how you feel... people who have been and still are in the boat you are in now. It is critical you get that support."

Her advice was to join a group called Compassionate Friends, a national support group for parents who had lost children.

I listened to Lois because I knew she was well qualified to give advice to me about losing a child violently.

The previous year her sixteen-year-old daughter had been walking home from high school when she was kidnapped by two men, dragged into the woods, tortured, raped and then murdered.

I was horrified when I heard about it and I went to the wake but did not know what to say to her. She and her husband appeared to be very strong, but looks I knew could be deceptive, because her husband died three months after his daughter was killed was killed and Lois believed that the stress of the murder was more than he could deal with.

So, I knew that Lois knew all about horror, grief and the effects it had on the mind. She had become an expert at that.

Lois said that everyone involved with Compassionate Friends had lost a child, and all members rally around a new member and provide all the support that this member needs.

"You can talk freely there and everyone will listen to your story, even if you tell it over and over again. Their greatest value is their ability to listen."

Lois had other advice to give us about how to go about coping with the tragedy and how to handle our relations with our friends and neighbors who had no idea about what we were going through.

The most useful information was her advice to find a person among our friends or relatives who was a good listener, and to call this person whenever one of us felt like talking about Padraic, and to avoid talking about him to people who could not handle the situation.

"People expect you to mourn for a short period of time and then get over it. They believe that life must go on and that you must pick up the pieces. Your obvious grieving will be an embarrassment to most people. Most of them will never talk to you about your son again, and they will think that you are being very insensitive if you bring his name up. That, unfortunately, is the way people are.

"And yet for a long time to come your son's death will be all that is on your mind and you will be compelled to talk about him no matter what others think of you.

"It is for this reason that you should join a local chapter of Compassionate Friends. When you are with the group you can vent your feelings at any time and can find comfort in the knowledge that you are not alone.

"But you will not find a cure for your grief there—you will just find some tools to cope with your grief."

Lois gave the address and phone number of a group located near me in New Jersey, and told me to talk her suggestion over with Eileen.

"You may not like going to these meetings, or Eileen may not like the meetings either, and if this is the case do not go. They are not for everybody. But give it a try. You have nothing to lose."

I took Lois Bohevesky's advice and for the next several years we found a haven where I could talk about my loss with new friends from Compassionate Friends.

We even went to conventions around the country, in Omaha and Florida, and we were able to bring Nora with us, because there were programs at those conventions for grieving children and Nora found them useful.

Eileen came with me to a number of the meetings, but she was not comfortable venting her grief to relative strangers and preferred to talk to a few close friends instead. So, I would sometimes go alone.

Our approach to grieving was in many ways typical of married couples, because there is no right or wrong way to grieve and each individual has to find a way to handle the grief in a manner that is most comfortable.

Padraic's death drew Eileen closer to our Church, and for many years she read and cherished a copy of the Good News Bible, which Padraic had used at school. She also attended Mass not only on Sundays but on many weekdays as well.

Padraic's death did not change my religious views one way or the other.

* * *

When the police lieutenant told me at the wake that the charges against the man who had been arrested for killing my son had been reduced I did not focus that much on the issue at that time because the wake and funeral was all that I could focus on. But after the funeral this was an issue that I made a priority.

The police had charged him with vehicular homicide after his arrest, which could have got the driver ten years in jail, but the District Attorney's office lowered the charges to leaving the scene of an accident, because the attorney believed he did not have enough witnesses to get a conviction. Leaving the scene of an accident merited only thirty days in jail at that time in New Jersey, even when there was a fatality involved. The laws have changed since then.

In Padraic's case, he had crossed a two-lane highway on a skateboard on his way to a nearby shopping center and he did not have the green light to make the crossing.

There was a car approaching on the inside lane towards him traveling within the 35-mile per hour speed limit, and he apparently thought he had plenty of time to get across, because the car was hundreds of yards down the road.

But Padraic apparently did not see a second car traveling on the outside lane doing sixty miles an hour, because the first car probably hid it from Padraic's view, and when Padraic was out in the middle of the road the car ploughed into him, tossing him like a rag doll onto the side of the road and breaking almost every bone in his body.

The car's windshield was broken and the driver got out briefly and looked at Padraic's body, then he got into his car and sped away.

The driver might have got away completely with this crime were it not for the fact that another driver jotted down his license plate, called the police, and the driver was arrested in New York City the following morning. The car with the broken windshield was in the driveway, and when the police went into the man's apartment they found a book of Yellow Pages on the kitchen table open at the section for windshields.

Obviously he had no intention of taking responsibility for my son's death.

The police did an investigation of the driver who turned out to be a 22-year-old Greek national named Christodoulou who had over-stayed his visa, and he was driving a car with no insurance and no registration.

It could not be determined at first who owned the car, but later it turned out he was working for a Greek company that exported used American cars abroad, and this car could have been one of them, but prior ownership could not be determined because the identification numbers had been filed down.

The driver said he had bought the car for $10,000 cash from another Greek who had left the country, but he could not produce receipts. He could not explain either where he got the $10,000 in cash in the first place.

His employer said he knew nothing about the car. He said Christodoulou was just a part-time worker and he knew nothing about his private affairs.

We got a call from a neighbor who said that the driver had been in a neighborhood bar for several hours before the accident and when I checked with the bartender he told me that the Greek was a regular and had numerous whiskeys there that night before he drove away.

I told this to the police, but they told me that this could not be used as evidence against him because he had fled the scene and there was no way to prove he had been drunk behind the wheel.

The police said it would be pointless to give him a blood test the following day because he could say he had a number of drinks after the accident to calm his nerves.

The police continued to assure me that if they had any say in the matter the driver would face a whole range of charges, but it was the district attorney's decision and there was nothing they could do about it.

I attended the trial of the driver and for the first time looked at the person who was the last to see Padraic alive before he plowed into him with his car.

He was a stocky man with a bloated drinker's face and he was very nervous as he walked into the courtroom accompanied by his lawyer. He walked right by me without trying to make any eye contact.

His lawyer began the proceedings by stating that his client had decided to plead guilty to leaving the scene of an accident, which was all he was being charged with. The judge accepted the plea, which carried a maximum sentence of thirty days in jail.

I watched this man, who's drinking and speeding had killed my son and created havoc in our family, and wondered how a legal system could not hold him accountable for his actions.

I understood that Padraic had shared some of the blame for his own death by not waiting for a green light before he crossed the street, but at the same time I was convinced that the district attorney could have at least tried to acquire some witnesses that would testify to Christodoulou's excessive drinking and speeding and make an effort to do a complete investigation of the incident.

Christodoulou's lawyer's strategy was to try and get his client a suspended sentence or a fine, instead of the thirty day jail sentence he was facing. So, he made a passionate plea to the judge about his client, who he claimed was a decent young man, who was the son of a Greek general, and who had never been in trouble with the law before and who had made a terrible mistake. He said he left the scene of the accident because he had overstayed his visa and he thought he would go to jail for that. The lawyer claimed that Padraic had collided with his client's car and there was no way he could have avoided him. The lawyer also said his client was devastated by the death of the teenager, and that he would give his own life if he could bring the boy back to life again.

The lawyer begged the judge not to put his client in jail with criminals, because he was not a criminal.

The prosecutor argued for a jail sentence by saying that Christodoulou's conduct was inexcusable: he had run into a child and left him dying on the side of the road without making any attempt to help him. And he showed by fleeing the scene that he had no intention of taking any responsibility for his actions.

The prosecutor made no mention of the drunken driving because he could not prove it. He made no mention of the speeding because the witness who said he saw Christodoulou speeding refused to testify. He did not mention that there was no evidence to show who owned the car; that there was no insurance on the car; that the driver could not produce a driver's license; or that he was an illegal alien.

And he would tell me later that that the only items that could be introduced to the judge were those items that were relevant to the charge of leaving the scene of an accident.

The judge listened to the evidence and then gave Christodoulou thirty days in jail, but watered down the sentence to make it meaningless. The defense lawyer asked that his client be allowed to serve his sentence on weekends, because he was attending college in Queens, NY, and did not want to interrupt his studies. This would amount to fifteen weekends.

The judge went along with this and allowed him to begin his weekend sentence on a Saturday afternoon and end it on a Sunday evening, thereby getting credit for two days in jail while serving only one night and one and one quarter days in jail.

Then he was given credit for three days he spent in jail between his arrest and being granted bail, which knocked two weekends off his fifteen weekend sentence. Then there would be an allowance for good behavior which would chop off another four weekends of the sentence, and a further four weekends off as a suspended sentence because he was a first time offender.

Thus, out of the fifteen weekends supposed to have been served, only five were served, which totaled five Saturday nights and seven days in jail.

I was infuriated at the sentence.

I knew that the prosecutor had a great deal to do with this sentence for two reasons. First of all he made no objections to the concessions the defense lawyer was winning from the judge, and secondly he had told me before the sentencing that that my son had crossed the road without having a green light and his behavior had contributed to the accident.

"I can well understand the panic that would lead a driver to flee the scene when he saw the victim was a child."

I told him I wanted to meet with him in his office and discuss the case because I wanted an explanation why he "understood" the panic of a drunken driver who had just made a mistake, and why he believed the defendant had paid sufficiently for his mistake with this sentence.

I said Padraic was just a child who also made a mistake that thousands of people in the city make every day of the week – crossing against a traffic light -- but he had paid for this mistake with his life.

Did the prosecutor understand why we believed the sentence was not acceptable? Christodoulou could be charged with having no license, no insurance, no title to the car, lying to the police, being drunk while driving. The prosecutor could ask Immigration to arrest him for being illegal, ask the FBI to investigate the status of the car with the vehicle identification number erased. Was the prosecutor going to let him walk away?

The answer was yes, he was going to let him walk away because he had bigger fish to fry. There was gang warfare in the streets, there were cases of corruption to be investigated, and he had no intention on spending any more resources on a case that was basically a traffic accident.

"I have no evidence for any of the issues you are bringing up and I have not got the staff to develop it. This case is done. Over."

The prosecutor was obviously annoyed at me. He said he was presently working on a case where a man walked into a bar and shot another man in the back of the head and killed him.

"You cannot compare that crime to your situation. The driver did not mean to kill your son; the other man meant to kill his victim. There is a world of difference."

I told him I disagreed with him. Both crimes led to deaths. My son was as dead as if he had been shot.

I also pointed out that anyone who gets into a car while drunk has a weapon under his control that is as deadly as a pistol—that more people are killed each year by drunken drivers than by people using guns.

But the prosecutor was not just interested in pursuing other aspects of the case: namely, the police opinion that the car was stolen; the police opinion that the driver might be part of a ring that smuggled stolen cars out of the United States to sell them in Africa; or the fact that the driver was in the country illegally. He was just not interested.

So, I abandoned any hope that the prosecutor would make Christodoulou pay for his behavior. He seemed to be home free.

Several months later I tried to sue him for damages, but my lawyer told me that he had no assets and no insurance, so what would be the point in suing him. I told the lawyer to file a suit anyway, but Christodoulou refused to respond and ignored all communications. The car involved in the case was confiscated by the state because no ownership could be proved.

I approached the FBI in Newark and let them know about the possibility that there was a criminal ring operating in Jersey City that was shipping stolen cars abroad, but I was told that unless I brought in proof of this nothing could be done. It seems that the FBI had such a mountain of possible criminal cases that they could pursue that they always pursued the most high profile cases and couldn't be bothered becoming involved in minor allegations based on rumor.

I had a friend who worked for Immigration and I asked him why Christodoulou was not arrested and deported, and he told me that his smart lawyer had probably had filed an appeal with Immigration about getting a Permanent Resident Visa, and that the appeal could take years to wind its way through the Immigration process, and that we would never be deported while that process was ongoing.

I brought up the conviction for leaving the scene of a fatal accident? He said that did not rise to the level of moral degradation that would trigger a deportation!
As for the rest of the issues: the stolen car, the drinking, the refusing to help a dying child; this could not be brought up because Christodoulou was not charged with any of this, so Immigration, like the FBI, had no interest in the case.

Christodoulou had got away with it.

* * *

There are two phrases that always make their appearance in the media coverage in the aftermath of a tragedy, which probably makes a great deal of sense to the journalist who use those phrases, but make no sense at all to a parent who has lost a child. These two phrases are "The need for closure" and "The healing has begun."

For instance, the day after the recent massacre in a church in Charleston, South Carolina, there was widespread coverage in the media about closure and healing, as if either could be achieved in a matter of days. The reality is that the families of the victims will experience healing and closure only with the passage of a very long time, especially those who lost a son or daughter, and for some there will never be either healing or closure.

The killing of Padraic has affected the Campbell family in many different ways.

If a tragedy occurs, such as a murder, or a horrendous accident, we immediately understand the grief of the relatives, and know exactly how they are feeling.

I watched the destruction of the Challenger Space Shuttle on January 28, 1986, seven weeks after the death of Padraic, and saw my own grief reflected on the faces of the parents of some of the dead astronauts.

The President of the United States spoke of dead heroes at the memorial services for the astronauts and said that the healing was beginning, but the shock on the faces of the parents, wives and children told another story—that healing or closure was a long way off.

I was in the World Trade Center Lobby in February, 1993, when a truck bomb went off in the basement below the lobby, and several hours later watched as five dead bodies of my Port Authority colleagues were carried through the lobby and out to waiting ambulances. One was a pregnant women, and I heard the director of the World Trade Center ask for volunteers to bring the terrible news to the woman's husband. It brought back memories of two policemen coming to my home on December 5, 1985, to tell me my son was dead, killed by a car whose driver had run off and left him dying on the roadside. I shuddered as I thought of the horror that awaited the dead women's spouse.

I was at Newark Airport in 2003 waiting to board a United flight to Dublin, when hundreds of young American soldiers came into the terminal full of youth and excitement because they were going on a charter flight to Iraq. They obviously were thrilled at the possibility of "action", but I could only wonder how many of them would die over there and would come back in a box to grieving parents. I had sympathy for the parents, and animosity towards the politicians who would put these youngsters in harm's way.

Most people are not so tuned in to the survivors of tragedy as we are. The unique mental storm brought on by the death of a child brings on a sensitivity that lasts for a lifetime.

* * *

In recent years, however, Eileen and I have been given what seems to be like a second chance.

Nora grew up to be a talented, stable young woman in spite of the tragedy she experienced when she was eight, a tragedy that was catastrophic for her, because Padraic, who was five years older than her, always looked out for her. She went on to graduate from the University of Pennsylvania and while there met her husband Joseph Bernard Fitzpatrick III.

After graduating she joined the Federal Reserve Bank of New York. She is now an officer there.

In December 2003, eighteen years after Padraic's death she gave birth to a beautiful boy, Joseph Bernard Fitzpatrick IV. The day he was born I felt a sense of renewal...a sense that I had another chance to love a child...and I could see my joy reflected in Eileen, who absolutely adored the little boy.

On August 29, 2005, Nora gave birth to a beautiful little girl named Eileen Teresa Fitzpatrick, and our joy knew no bounds.

And in the years that followed three more grandchildren arrived, Timothy, Genevieve and Daniel, and our lives have been enriched by every one of these children.

Neither Eileen nor I see our wonderful grandchildren as replacements for Padraic, because Padraic is irreplaceable.

However, we both have learned by the arrival of our grandchildren that even after a great tragedy it is possible to find joy in life once again and enter into the type of relationship with children that makes life worthwhile.

* * *

Campbell Family (1977)

Padraic (1980)

Nora (1984)

Padraic, shortly before his death (1985)

Nora, track star (1987)

Nora and Trey Fitzpatrick

Wedding in Ireland (2001)

The Fitzpatrick Children

Genevieve, Joseph, Daniel, Nellie

and Timothy (2015)

CPSIA information can be obtained
at www.ICGtesting.com
Printed in the USA
LVOW04s2149080516
487235LV00056B/467/P